Henry Ware Putnam

Oration Delivered Before the City Council and Citizens of

Boston

On the one hundred and seventeenth anniversary of the Declaration of

Independence July 4, 1893

Henry Ware Putnam

Oration Delivered Before the City Council and Citizens of Boston
*On the one hundred and seventeenth anniversary of the Declaration of
Independence July 4, 1893*

ISBN/EAN: 9783337301071

Printed in Europe, USA, Canada, Australia, Japan

Cover: Foto ©ninafisch / pixelio.de

More available books at **www.hansebooks.com**

ORATION

DELIVERED BEFORE THE

CITY COUNCIL AND CITIZENS

OF

BOSTON

ON THE

ONE HUNDRED AND SEVENTEENTH ANNIVERSARY OF THE DECLARATION OF INDEPENDENCE

JULY 4, 1893

BY

HENRY W. ⎞PUTNAM, Esq.

SICUT PATRIBUS, SIT DEUS NOBIS

BOSTONIA
CONDITA Æ.
1630.

CIVITATIS REGIMINE DONATA AD. 1822.

BOSTON
PRINTED BY ORDER OF THE CITY COUNCIL
1893

CITY OF BOSTON.

In Board of Aldermen, July 5, 1893.

Resolved, That the thanks of the City Council be expressed to Henry W. Putnam, Esq., for the patriotic and eloquent Oration delivered by him before the city authorities on the Fourth of July, in commemoration of the One Hundred and Seventeenth Anniversary of American Independence; and that he be requested to furnish a copy thereof for publication.

Adopted unanimously. Sent down for concurrence.

JOHN H. LEE,
Chairman.

In Common Council, September 21, 1893.
Concurred unanimously, by a rising vote.

DAVID F. BARRY,
President.

Approved September 27, 1893.

N. MATTHEWS, JR.,
Mayor.

A true copy.

Attest:

J. M. GALVIN,
City Clerk.

THE MISSION OF OUR PEOPLE.

Mr. Mayor and Fellow-Citizens:

The time-honored celebration of Independence Day by publicly reading the immortal declaration in the city of Faneuil Hall and the Old State House, of the Old South and the Boston Massacre, of Bunker Hill and Dorchester Heights, and on this spot but a step from where the Liberty Tree stood, has a significance which similar observances cannot have elsewhere, even in Philadelphia. For it was in our dear old rebellious town that the fires of liberty were kindled and kept aglow until the bolt was forged and welded and driven home. Others elsewhere may equally appreciate the historical importance of the great event and of the principles then proclaimed, and be equally grateful for its beneficent results to posterity; but every Boston man carries the old Revolutionary spirit in his blood in his daily walks through our storied streets. It is his daily bread, his personal and domestic affair. A single spark, and the old flame blazes up in a moment with all its early glow and fervor. Thus may it ever be! Times and popular habits may change, and do indeed change rapidly; but so long as constitutional freedom reigns in the land may the glorious, familiar story be rehearsed to the hurrying generations on this anniversary in the old historic town of Sam Adams and the Sons of Liberty!

If we turn from the external side of our Fourth of July celebrations, — from the scream of the eagle, the waving of the flag, the ringing of the bells, and that most exquisitely native New England feature, which we have ever with us, the Chinese cracker and the Roman fire-work, — we find even within quite recent times a great change in the attitude of thougtful people towards the day and towards the event it commemorates. As that event is looked at through the lengthening vista of the years, and especially through the medium of national convulsions like the War of the Rebellion, its importance, indeed, does not diminish, but our historical perspective is enlarged and we see things more in their true proportions. It used to seem as if the world began with our national independence, and as if the American

Republic sprang full-grown and perfect from the front of Jove by a creative fiat; the millennium had come all at once; there had been no before, and there would be no serious hereafter to reckon with. It is true, our national tone of confidence and glorification was pitched a little high and shrill, as if we had some misgiving, a lurking distrust that all was not well; and it was not until the gigantic struggle with slavery had been successfully met that the key was lowered and we adopted the soberer tone that goes with mature life and with the consciousness of the dangers that beset the path of nations and of our ability under God to overcome them.

In this frame of mind, and looking back into the stored wisdom of the past for guiding principles to deal thoughtfully with the thronging questions of the present, our point of view has changed. We see more clearly than before that the principles and deeds of 1776 form but one link in a long chain of historic events which have made us what we are. Our mere political independence of Great Britain is, in this view, a trifling matter compared with the common interests of law, trade, language, political principles and habits, race sympathy and mission, in which the branches of the English-speaking races are united and mutually dependent. How much more closely inter-dependent, for instance, are we with England to-day, though politically separate, than were our colonial fathers, even before so much as the first sign of serious discord with the mother-country had appeared on the horizon! As we glance back over the majestic current of English history and English law, rising in the dim distance of Roman institutions and Teutonic customs, and follow it down through the times of the great lawgivers and epoch-making rulers, of Alfred, William of Normandy, and Edward I., of Elizabeth, Cromwell, and William III., of Magna Charta, the foundation of the House of Commons, the petitions of right, the struggle over ship-money, the Puritan Commowealth, how fatuous seems the attempt of a dull and obstinate old Hanoverian tyrant to tax the colonists in defiance of the ancient English principles of right and against the convictions and protests of the great Englishmen of his own time, — the Chathams, the Foxes, the Burkes! As the centuries move on, will this effort of a narrow-minded, alien, and absolutist king, sitting upon the throne of Alfred, a monarch who knew less of the funda-

mental Anglo-Saxon principles of law and government than any tapster in his realm, create so
much as a ripple on that great human stream
of unity and progress which the English-speaking races are pouring out in the United States,
Canada, the Maritime Provinces, Australia, —
wherever in the broad world the American or
the British flag is carried? Our fathers were
but own brothers of the blood to the barons
that vindicated the personal liberty of the subject at Runnymede; to the knights that fought
with de Montfort at Evesham, and sealed forever with their blood and his the right of the
humblest burgher and tradesman in a land of
privilege to sit in Parliament and vote on the
taxes he was to pay; to the Commoners who
fought Charles Stuart to the block ere he
should govern and tax by the royal prerogative
alone. More far-reaching, indeed, in its im-
mediate results was their work than that of
their elder brothers in freedom, for it founded
a new polity on a virgin soil where the latent
forces of democracy in the world should take
root and grow beyond the dream of the statesman or the philosopher; but all these great
deeds were essentially equals, that of our fathers
merely *primus inter pares.* The independent

federal republic is but the sumptuous frame in
which our own noble canvas is set; the strong
lines, the glowing colors, the splendid figures, the
stirring and dramatic groups, the historic back-
ground, in which the picture of the growth of
liberty is drawn, are the same and incomparable
in them all. It cannot be wholly the bias in
the blood which pronounces this stately march
of the race to universal freedom and almost
boundless empire, to be the foremost movement in
human history and one whose possibilities are
hardly hinted at by what we see already
achieved about us in the world to-day.

But while this grand thought is at once the
comfort and the inspiration of the English-speaking millions and of their adopted fellow-citizens,
and above all, ours, who stand in the van of
the great march, and while it might well form
the sole theme of a Fourth of July oration,
still the growth of empire has brought with it
the perplexities, the dangers of empire; and in
these latter days, when we gather on formal
occasions, we are more apt to take counsel together on the problems of the present than
merely to glory in the achievements of the past
or in the millennium that is coming. Those
problems loom up dark and numerous enough, —

a noisome brood. A shifting and dishonest currency, offering a fraction in payment where the whole is honestly earned, and threatening our whole financial system with dishonor and disaster; the strongly-entrenched perversion of government taxation from the raising of necessary revenue to the emolument of the favored few at the expense of the consuming many; a pension-list swollen to uncounted and ever-growing millions of money, making peace more expensive and more demoralizing than war and converting the nation's roll of honor into a sordid list of grabbers at the government's money-bags; paternalism, and its twin sister and handmaiden socialism, sapping the energy and self-reliance of the people, turning government into an end itself instead of a means, threatening the fundamental personal freedom of the individual, and even the right of private property; labor and capital arrayed in armed camps and unceasing war against each other, each seemingly bent on the other's ruin; accumulations of corporate wealth seeking by every astute and hidden device to extort from the toiling and preoccupied masses an exorbitant return upon a fictitious capital; great cities sinking in the mire of corruption as they grow larger and more heterogeneous in their population; the terrible frequency and impunity of homicidal crime and the defiant misuse of the pardoning power in favor of red-handed murderers of the officers of the law; alien races, seemingly almost incapable of assimilation with our political or social systems, seeking in unlimited numbers the untrammelled and irresponsible enjoyment of both; and the line could be stretched out to the crack of doom. Here is enough, and to spare, to rejoice the hearts of all the Jeremiahs and Cassandras of the country and of the world, and to keep them busy the rest of their natural lives. But the patriotic American is happily neither a Jeremiah nor a Cassandra. There is no place among us for the mere croaker or the mere prophet of ill; he is a man without a country and is left severely alone or shown courteously to the door, and asked to take his peculiar note elsewhere. If he insists upon staying he must register and take out a proper certificate so that he can be identified by the police on pain of being "deported" to his native land, — if the latter can be found.

The American citizen, although constitutionally confident and optimistic to a fault, thinks and acts more on the problems of his country and of his time than the individual citizen of any state has ever done before. The genius of his institutions requires this of him; if they are to fulfil their entire mission his participation in public affairs has got to become even more general, more active, and more effective. For one, I am convinced that, in a thousand different and often inconspicuous ways, it is constantly becoming so in the formation and enforcement of public opinion. Not the least gratifying sign of the times in this connection is the fact that the observance of Independence Day has become more thoughtful than formerly and more concerned with the practical questions of the present than with the glories of the past or with mere noise and parade. Let us briefly look at one or two of our current problems for a few moments.

Prominent among the articles of indictment against old King George inserted by our fathers in the Declaration of Independence which our eloquent young friend has just read, is this: "For cutting off our trade with all parts of the world." It is a part of the bitter irony of history that the fabric which they carefuly and toilfully, with tears and blood, built upon this foundation-stone has by force of circumstances become a more effective barrier to "our trade with all parts of the world" than all the Navigation Acts which Stuarts and Hanoverians had for a hundred years loaded upon the backs of the patient colonists. Within a century the country whose founders recognized the free interchange of commodities with foreign nations as one of the fundamental blessings which civilized man should fight for rather than go without it, came to be the foremost representative in the civilized world of the opposite idea that foreign trade is a natural evil to be avoided altogether or reduced to its lowest terms. The little group of colonies strung along the Atlantic seaboard, with a jealous mother-country over-sea in front, and hostile French and Indians in the backwoods behind, was broad, catholic, cosmopolitan, far-sighted; the great imperial Republic, stretching from sea to sea, powerful and respected at home and abroad, with nothing to fear from anybody, at peace with all the world, teaming with an active and intelligent population and with the unbounded resources of a continent, is narrow, exclusive, provincial, afraid of the healthy competition of the world in trade; shuts its ports as tight as it can, as if forsooth it could sell its own surplus products without buying those of the rest of the world. By what strange jugglery of historic forces has a powerful nation voluntarily and deliberately laid upon its own neck a yoke which the proud monarchy of England could not maintain upon the necks of the feeble and straggling colonists, and driven from the sea its own ships which the Crown with the whole Royal Navy could not do before? By what series of steps, each no doubt a logical and necessary one at the time when it was taken, have we been led to reverse completely the maxim of the founders, and, ourselves, by our own act, unaided and alone, almost to " cut off our trade with all parts of the world " ?

This is no occasion for discussing any strictly political or partisan topic. On the question of protection and free trade, the people of the country are divided into two great opposing camps of opinion, equally honest, equally intelligent, equally patriotic, about equal in numbers, all of them true Americans; as an economic question on which political parties divide and contend, we cannot, and we would not, discuss it on our national day. But if we detect a national tendency or trend of thought toward a cardinal principle of the founders, a veering of the ship of state back towards a course from which eddies and counter-currents, misleading lights and darkness and the tempest of war, had turned her, we may note it as we pass.

If there be a single trait of the Anglo-Saxon race more characteristic of it than its passionate love of freedom and its mission as a lawgiver and founder of states, that trait is its genius for commerce, its passion for the romance. of the sea, its love of the trackless ocean as the pathway for the exchange of commodities between the nations of the world. It is almost as certain that an English-speaking nation will not give up, except temporarily and in obedience to some overruling necessity of the moment, its unrestrained freedom of trade, as it is that it will not surrender the principles of Magna Charta, the Bill of Rights, and the Habeas Corpus. The history of foreign commerce has been the history of discovery, of the advance of civilization, of the expanding brotherhood and progress of mankind. A manner of raising the means for carrying on goverment cannot permanently prevail which has for one of its chief objects the extinction or discredit of that very branch of human activity which has done most to discover new lands and found new states, and for the

prosecution of which, with the blessings it brings
in its train, human governments are largely or-
ganized and carried on. It would almost pass
human belief that a shrewd and inventive, as
well as free, people should long adhere to a
manner of raising their national revenue which
is not only adverse to " trade with all parts of
the world," but whose aim and tendency are
artificially to enhance the price of foreign articles or similar ones produced here so as to
make them cost more to ourselves than they
otherwise would.

Is, then, the high-tariff system, which has for
its object primarily not revenue but protection
against foreign products, being now maintained
by its advocates as a finality, to be defended
as a cardinal principle and to be fought for as
an article of faith ; or is their advocacy of it
merely from that conservative instinct which
seeks to avert all sudden and revolutionary
change and which ensures thorough discussion
and gradual adaptation of vested interests to
new conditions before any change is made ?
It seems to me that the latter is the case, and
that two instances, — one from the philosophical
side, and one, very recent, from the peculiarly
practical side, — have a strong tendency to prove

that it is. By the former I mean our second martyred chief magistrate, who is enshrined in the hearts of his countrymen as well as impressed upon their minds as no other deceased statesman of our time is except our first martyr in the Presidency. It is well known that President Garfield, himself the titular as well as the intellectual leader, at the time, of the party of high protection, said that all modifications of the tariff should be made with a view to ultimate free trade, and that every step taken should lead in that direction. My second instance is that of a prominent business man, a representative American in energy, thrift, enterprise, and success in the accumulation of wealth, and a peculiarly typical beneficiary of the high protective system. In a recent interesting Utopian paper upon the proposed reunion of all the English-speaking nations of the globe under one government, Mr. Andrew Carnegie dwells upon the free trade which would practically result from such a confederation as one of the chief attractions of his plan, and says that such manufacturing interests throughout our land as he represents in his own person would welcome the change. I quote his words: "I do not shut my eyes to the fact that reunion, bringing free en-

trance of British products, would cause serious
disturbance to many manufacturing interests near
the Atlantic coast which have been built up
under the protective system. But, sensitive as
the American is said to be to the influence of
the dollar, there is a chord in his nature — the
patriotic — which is much more sensitive still.
Judging from my knowledge of the American
manufacturers there are few who would not
gladly make the necessary pecuniary sacrifices
to bring about a reunion of the old home and
the new. There would be some opposition of
course from those pecuniarily interested, but this
would be silenced by the chorus of approval
from the people in general. No private interests,
or interests of a class, or of a section of what
would then be our common country, would or
should be allowed to obstruct a consummation so
devoutly to be wished."

That is nobly spoken, and like a patriotic
American. It is true that Mr. Carnegie proposes
political reunion with England and her world-
wide dependencies as a condition of establishing
free trade, and puts his proposition in the form
of a concession to sentiment. But can the pecuniary sacrifice which he and the other specially favored beneficiaries of protection would be

willing to make for mere sentiment be, even temporarily, a very serious one? It certainly is the general impression that those for whom he professes to speak are not, as a class, prone to give up large material advantages for sentiment alone. Nor is it to be supposed for a moment that as patriotic American citizens Mr. Carnegie and his friends seriously think that the great triumphant Republic is to gain much politically either in knowledge, principles, or practice, by reunion with the monarchy, or that our patriotic sentiment could then be of a higher order than the one we now have for the stars and stripes, or command higher sacrifices. The work of the fathers, cemented and developed by the sons during the century, puts us far in the van of the modern world as the builders of states, and makes us stand towards the rest of the world as teachers rather than learners, as leaders rather than followers. Surely no higher patriotism can be imagined than our love for our Union, nor one for which greater sacrifices should be made. No; neither patriotic sentiment, nor the political advantage to us of the proposed confederation, can account for the willingness to accept unrestricted trade or be the real ground for it; these can be little more than the convenient

pretexts, put forward for consistency's sake, to
make easier the transition from a system whose
beneficiaries themselves feel that the change must
come before long, and will in the end be to the
advantage of all. When that change comes, —
whether sooner or later, in this decade, or the
next, or the following, — when the perplexing
problem of raising a nation's necessary revenue
is reconciled with the great principle of unham-
pered trade, when our sails again whiten every
sea and our flag is seen in every port, and all
the good things which the bounty of God and
the skill and industry of man can produce
throughout the earth are poured into our laps
without hostile barrier to exclude or artificial
enhancement of price, then will be grandly real-
ized the dream of the signers of the great Declaration for " trade with all parts of the world "
and the blessings that will follow in its path.

Turn with me, for a moment, to another important problem of the day, the government of
cities. Hardly anything would, I think, have
surprised the founders of the Republic more than
to be told that within a century America would
become a by-word throughout the civilized world
for monstrous and even grotesque misgovernment of large cities. It is true that they had

no large cities themselves and had little idea of
the enormous immigration of foreigners, unac-
quainted with the principles or practice of self-
government, which was to pour in upon us like
a flood and settle down to urban life in our
midst; but if they had, they would probably not
have expressed a doubt, any more than they
actually did, as to the entire ability of the
people to grapple promptly with the problem
as it arose and solve it out of hand. It was
taken for granted,. as an axiom, that local government would take care of itself as a matter of
course; that it was only necessary to erect the
colonies into States and to unite the States in
a strong and well-adjusted federal bond, and the
whole work of government was done. Many of the
Revolutionary statesmen were profoundly distrust-
ful of the permanent success of the Union; all had
misgivings and forebodings lest the levelling democracy of the masses or the strong hand of the
usurper might ere long bring the work of their
lives to naught; some went to their graves,
even many years after the adoption of the Con-
stitution, with the thought weighing upon their
souls that the Union might not long survive
the war of factions and of party passion. But
did one of them even dream that, though the

splendid apex of the pyramid, soaring to the
clouds, should stand the shock of storms and
the wear of time and grow only firmer and more
lustrous under both, that the broad, solid base
would corrode and rot and the whole structure
be undermined and weakened where it was
throught to be unassailably strong? They fore-
saw nearly all the dangers that in fact have
from time to time beset the federal Union, and
many which have not arisen at all, but it
seems hardly to have occurred to them that
trouble could arise at the very homes and hearth-
stones of the people, where the citizen was close
at hand and personally present to watch and
control the course of affairs. Representative
rule on a large scale, at a distant capital, under
a dual system of government, and with a population scattered over an immense territory, was
indeed an experiment about which they might
have grave and anxious doubts; but local rule
by the people at their own doors, — had not
centuries of experience shown that honest, effi-
cient, and economical home-rule in local affairs
was the one unvarying, unquestioned achievement
of the race? Could the time ever come when
the ablest and most thoughtful men in the com-
munity would lack either the public spirit, the

ability, or the proper machinery of government
to make themselves felt effectively in controlling
the administration of local affairs, and would surrender it to men seeking only their own personal
advantage at the expense of the general good?

This question, which our fathers had not to
deal with, now confronts us as a problem of
vast import; for nothing in the future is surer
than the continued growth in number and
population of our large cities, and far the
greater number of points at which government
touches the pocket or the person of the citizen
must always be in the matters of municipal,
rather than of state or national, administration.
The success of state and national government,
too, is inevitably at stake, in the long run, on
the success of municipal government, for if the
trunk is girdled at the base it cannot be long
before the tree with its blossoms, its fruit, and
its gracious shade will fall. Already we have
seen in some parts of our country the corrupt
political machinery of great cities controlling and
debauching the administration of States, and in
one case at least reaching out defiantly, and not
without prospect of success, to seize the Presidency itself. If we fail in local self-government
the whole experiment of democracy ultimately

fails. We may turn at times to the State for
purification and relief in local administration, but
it is obvious that such resort can be only tem-
porary and transient. The fountain can rise no
higher than its source, and if local sources are
polluted it can only be a short time before the
main stream becomes helplessly impure. The
State, as the creator of corporations, furnishes
the legal machinery and modifies it from time
to time as needed, but it can, in the long run,
do no more, and in any healthy condition of
public affairs the administration of local affairs
must be by local authorities responsible to a
local constituency which jealously watches and
sternly enforces that responsibility. Thus, and
not otherwise, can our whole political system be
kept sound at the core ; and so long as the
core is sound — and so long only — will the
tree flourish. Only very sparingly, upon the
simplest possible lines, in accordance with the
fundamental principles of home-rule, and when
the need of change is clear, should the inter-
vention of the State be exercised or invoked in
altering city charters ; otherwise popular confidence is shaken, our self-reliance is weakened,
popular indifference follows, new, complicated,
and unfamiliar machinery furnishes designing

men their opportunity, and then the worm is at
the root, and the blight must spread upward.
When we have adapted our city governments in
principle and in general form to that of our
confessedly successful national government, — a
single responsible executive elected by the
people, and a large and independent legislative
as broadly representative of the whole people
as it is practicable to make it, set over against
each. other with carefully distinguished separate
functions assigned to each, and have arranged
the administrative machinery in the simplest way
under the executive head, the State has done
all it can, except in the perfection and modi-
fication of details, to help us. The rest lies
with the people themselves in their several
localities, and the thorough and constant education of the people in the art of strictly local
self-government is the national, as well as local,
work before us ; for it is forever and unalter-
ably the theory and the corner-stone of republi-
can government that we are governed from
below upward, and that all our government,
like charity, begins at home.

It is worse than folly, it is suicide, to play
the pessimist and say that the problem of making cities govern themselves well is hopeless.

The highest intelligence, the best education, the
most enlightened public spirit, the most active
and thoughtful philanthropy, the highest business capacity and executive ability, are all of
them concentrated in cities, as well as the
worst ignorance, folly, and vice. Nowhere can
a sound public opinion form and organize so
easily, spread so quickly, and act so effectively
through the press and otherwise as in our cities,
and nowhere are reform movements of all kinds
so often and so successfully inaugurated. We
are certainly familiar enough with this in Boston. Have we not recently seen our own city
government put upon the statute book, and
keep there, a pioneer enactment in this Commonwealth, if not in the country, which strikes
at the very heart of the spoils system by for-
bidding the participation of municipal officers in
the machinery of political parties, a reform which
must soon be adopted for all other cities and
towns? And is it not at this moment a subject for patriotic pride that our city, under the
lead of its chief magistrate, and our Commonwealth by the action of its Legistature, have just
struck a telling and significant blow at that
corporate encroachment upon the fair rights of
the people, which is one of the worst and sub-

tlest dangers of the time, as of yore our fathers
struck at the Stamp Act and the Tea Tax? If
the powers of evil are concentrated and organ-
ized in cities as nowhere else, so also are the
powers of good, and nowhere can the battle between the two be fought out to so great advantage ; for the battlefield is at our very doors
and all can reach it and act upon it, in one
way or another, at the minimum of trouble and
expense. Our cities, as centres of the highest
education and intelligence, should become our
very best models of good government instead of
the reverse ; their misgovernment, where it has
not been already corrected, can be only a tem-
porary and transition state, destined to pass grad-
ually away as we face and grapple with the
conditions of the problem.

But how shall it be done? How shall the
ignorance and inertia of the great mass of the
people in regard to municipal government be
overcome, and the seemingly irresistible enginery
erected by sinister forces to turn local government largely to their own personal account be
destroyed or counteracted? How shall fraud,
jobbery, and waste be prevented, and the people
everywhere get a full and honest return for
every dollar they pay in taxes? Let us disa-

buse ourselves of all illusion or fatuity on this
subject. There is and can be no simple and com-
fortable answer to these questions; no patent
device for attaining our end; no short cut to
the goal we aim at. Nothing but a long,
patient, intelligent struggle will accomplish that
end, or maintain it after it is reached. The
fight must go on forever as our cities grow;
we can do little more, by legislation and political organization, than forge better weapons,
establish better discipline in the ranks, and maintain better outposts to prevent surprise and disaster; it remains for us still to make every
citizen a good soldier. When we have done all
that we can to get simple and effective municipal machinery that shall respond as quickly
and fully as may be to public opinion; when
we have developed the forces and means of
expression of that public opinion to their utmost;
when we have done our best to get good men
into office and to keep them there, and to keep
bad men out; when we have purified the ballot
and emancipated the civil service from the spoils-
man, we have done much, and we must keep on
doing it; but we have not touched the root of
the matter nor applied, scientifically, either the
necessary diagnosis or the final remedy.

It is a part of the inevitable logic of popular government that when it fails conspicuously at any point the disease must be one in the people as a whole. In the particular matter of local government it is obvious that our borders have so far filled up already — to say nothing of the future — that we can no longer run for luck, nor go by rule of thumb, nor trust wholly to the inspiration of the moment, or to the spasmodic or periodic uprisings of good men against misrule, or even to the educational influence upon municipal representatives and officers of public responsibility itself and of a free and vigilant public press. The foundations must be laid broad and deep, if reform is to be thorough and permanent and city government is to approach our ideal. The process can be no other than the slow, modest, painstaking, unsensational one of systematic school education. In a democracy, the boy's mind must, at the plastic age, be supplied with the rudiments of that science and art of government which he as a responsible sovereign is shortly to apply and practise, and above all, the correct point of view towards government must be indelibly impressed upon his mind and heart. Something is already done in the public schools in this line, chiefly with reference to the Con-

stitution of the United States and of the State;
but if a boy may well learn something about
the duties and functions of the President, the
members of the Cabinet, and the Senators and
members of Congress, shall he be taught nothing
about those of town-meetings and selectmen, of
county commissioners and surveyors of highways,
of the mayor, the departments, and the city council of his own city? Shall he learn about the
secretaries of State, War, and the Navy, the
treaty-making power, and the appointment and
duties of foreign ministers and counsels and the
justices of the Supreme Court, and not about
the great departments which protect his young
life from violence, fire, disease, and accident,
make his home, and the streets, parks, and
playgrounds safe and attractive for him, and
maintain the schools that educate him? Which
of the two touches him nearest and most directly?
Which will first confront him when he is a
voter, and is responsible for the wise and intelligent discharge of the duties of a citizen,
and which is his young mind capable of under-
standing most easily and studying to the best
advantage? Which really, and for all practical
purposes, has most to do with his life, liberty,
and the pursuit of happiness? If taught with

as little theory and with as much practical description as possible, which will be the most interesting to the boy? Why, in a few years, should not the very best of men for nearly every grade of municipal representative and employee be sought and found specially equipped for most of their work in the graduates of our schools? Why should not they have the honorable ambition as well as the conscious ability to do good municipal service however humble, and why should not the intelligent watchfulness of the great body of the voters over public servants be immeasurably increased by the same means? This strong leaven would soon pervade the whole body politic and improvement would be steady. To take an extreme, perhaps a fanciful, case, — the boys who were in the schools of New York when the Tweed *régime* was exposed and overthrown, and even those that were born during the next two or three years are now voters. If they and all that have been in those schools had been systematically instructed in the principles and some of the details of municipal government, impressed with its importance for the well-being of human society, and taught the duty of a voter, would not the prospects of that corruption-ridden city be, by this time, much less dark than they now are? And in what other way are they likely ever to become materially and permanently brighter?

We have reached the point where the public school and the private school and the institution of higher learning must everywhere take in hand vigorously and systematically the education of the future voter in the duties of citizenship in a free self-governing Republic, and at the very head of the list, because hitherto almost wholly neglected, because easiest for youth to understand, and because most vital and fundamental, I would put the duty of the voter and of the local officer to his city or town. Until we raise the rudiments of municipal government to that dignity we are rejecting the stone which should be the head of the corner and on which the whole fabric must eventually rest; while from the educational point of view we are, in the instruction of our youth, putting aside in this connection the concrete, the practical, the close at hand, the easily comprehensible, and teaching only the abstract, the theoretic, the remote, and to the young mind largely the unintelligible. The public school, especially, should, with its other duties, be the kindergarten of the young citizen, and its object-lessons should be taken from the home, the street, the playground, the public works and buildings, and the school itself.

But we should add to that, — what I have already alluded to as still more important, — instruction, or rather influence, as to the point of view from which the youth should look at the city or town in which he is shortly to assume the responsible duty of citizenship. We should inculcate the fundamental idea of citizenship, and of public office as a trust as sacred and inviolable as that between man and man or boy and boy. We should use every means to build up in the youth of our cities a sentiment which, for lack of a better name, I will call municipal patriotism or loyalty. The imagination must be touched and appealed to, and the city of his home should be idealized and personified to him, as his country already is, so that he shall not go out into life with the idea that the government of his city is an impersonal foreign corporation, naturally oppressive and hostile to his interests; which it is nobody's business to serve and protect; and which is fair game for everybody to get what he can out of. He should be made to feel, when an ingenuous,

impressionable boy at school, that the city is
his parent to whom he owes a filial and a loyal
service as he does to the flag of his country; that
to wrong her or let anybody else do so is as
despicable as to rob his sister, or brother, or
neighbor; that it is a proud and honorable duty
to render her the slightest faithful service. Let
the germs of civic pride be planted in the re-
sponsive young; let every patriotic chord of
history, of legend, of personal deeds, of civic,
military, and literary tradition, be touched and
played upon; let historic spots with great or
memorable associations be visited and their story
told, retold, and explained, until an honorable
local pride and ambition springs up that shall
inspire and elevate the character of the growing
citizen. There is certainly no municipality in
the land where this homely but important part
of a civic training could be so well inaugurated or
so fruitfully carried out as in our own historic
city, and with the youth that yearly swarm by
thousands into her hospitable schools; but there
is hardly a city or town in the land where it
cannot now be done, not one where it cannot
be done soon in these fast-moving days.

The grave difficulties thrown around the problem
of municipal government, and, indirectly, of all

government, by our inpouring foreign population
lead me to say a word about the question of
immigration before I sit down. If foreign trade
and local self-rule are two of the most marked
natural characteristics of our race, hardly less so
is our almost unlimited capacity for the absorption and assimilation of other races and the
transformation of them into our own general
type. Proud of our apparent mission to furnish
a free asylum to the unfortunate and oppressed,
and a fair field to the enterprising, of all races
and climes, and conscious of the strength and
elasticity of our institutions and of our social
order, we seem almost blind to the dangers at-
tending unrestricted immigration from across the
Atlantic, while we exaggerate those from the
direction of the Pacific. No thoughtful man
would probably deny that a far greater strain
has been put upon our institutions by the Anarchists of Chicago, the Mafia of New Orleans,
and the Tammany of New York, than by a few
thousand harmless, peaceable Chinese laborers
scattered over the land. As between the industrious and thrifty Mongolian laundry-man and
the hoodlums of whatever race extraction who
stone him because he is less afraid of work,
and less extortionate in his charge for it, than

they themselves are, who can hesitate in his choice? Cheap labor, if of good quality and accompanied with thrift, decency, and good citizenship, is like cheap goods, an unmixed boon, both moral and material, which should be encouraged and invited by every civilized nation. Yet all other foreign elements come to us almost without let or hindrance and seem likely to continue to do so, while we work ourselves into a panic about the Chinese, erect barriers against their coming, and even propose forcibly to deport those that are here.

I would not be understood as belittling the possible dangers of extensive Chinese immigration; on the contrary, I have a very strong feeling of sympathy with our fellow-citizens of the Pacific slope. We live in a glass house that makes it unsafe for us to throw many stones at them. They may well ask us when we are going to level our Chinese tariff-wall erected against harmless necessary coats, blankets, and cotton cloths, coal, iron, wool, and salt before we open the flood-gates of Mongolian immigration upon their defenceless heads. We must remember that they stand in the vanguard, upon the very picket-line, of the great advance of European civilization westward towards the

Orient. Across the broad, but ever-narrowing, Pacific, they gaze towards the restless, inscrutable, uncounted millions of Asia, alien, even antipodal, to us in race, religion, and civilization. They stand face to face with the same eternal Eastern Question which for twenty-five centuries has confronted Europe. What the Persian hosts were to Greece, what the Carthaginian armies were to Rome, what the Moors were to Spain, what the Ottoman Empire was and is to Eastern Europe, that the Chinese are, or seem, to our friends in California.

The resemblance may appear fanciful to us. We may feel that no sane man can see anything in the mild-mannered, industrious, law-abiding Chinese coming, even in large numbers, to our shores, at all like the armed hosts of Darius and Xerxes at Thermopylæ and Marathon, the Punic legions bringing the Roman State to the brink of ruin, the fierce Moslem hordes of Saracens and Turks overrunning south-western and south-eastern Europe with fire and sword and thundering at the very gates of Vienna. But the resemblance is closer than we think. It has not been war, in itself, that has so long made the Eastern Question menacing for Europe. On the contrary, war has often been the instrument for spreading the highest civilization. It was by war, and war alone, that Roman civilization was carried into Northern Europe, that Norman civilization was carried into Britain, that English civilization was spread over our own continent, displacing the native inhabitants. Nor, on the other hand, does the fact that the Chinese immigration is so peaceful and quiet make it necessarily harmless. We should not forget that, in the fulness of time, the peaceful importation by some traders of a few shiploads of African slaves brought the American Republic nearer to dissolution and ruin than the African phalanx of Hannibal — the veterans of a hundred fights, under a leader fired by an intense and lofty patriotism, and himself the most brilliant and indomitable captain of the ages — could bring the Republic of Rome. No; whether the Oriental comes with sword and spear or with flatiron and pick it is himself, his habits, his religion, and his social order that have ever been the stumbling-block, not the manner of his coming. An alien race in our midst, with us but not of us, is an inevitable peril to a government and to a social order in which all are to participate as sovereigns and as equals. In Europe, as with us, it has been the radical difference of race and civilization in each case

which has made the danger, — a danger in-
stinctively felt rather than clearly reasoned out,
but almost equally deep in each case.

We must free our minds from cant in both
directions on this question ; from the cant of
the mere humanitarian and theorizer as well as
from that of the demagogue of the sand-lots.
We may overwhelm a petty Geary Act with
our ridicule and contempt, as it richly deserves ;
but let us not be led away in our philan-
thropic zeal so far as to deny the right of
government, when not precluded by its own
treaties, to limit or forbid the immigration of
aliens or their deportation after they have immi-
grated. No more vital and fundamental principle
underlies all government than this right, and
no sounder or more salutary decision has ever
been rendered by the Supreme Court of the
United States than its recent vindication of our
right as a nation to protect our borders from
undesirable immigration and preserve from danger
what we have already achieved in building up a
government and a social order. It would be
well for us if the whole pestilent and blood-
stained horde of Anarchists, for instance, had
never been allowed to enter the country, or if
they should be deported now as public enemies

with the recreant Governor of Illinois at their head. They are outlaws, and have no place in the American Commonwealth.

The extent and manner in which such right shall be exercised will always be a delicate question, and the test must always be the purely practical one of expediency. The question must be, at any given moment, Have we so digested and assimilated what we have got that we can receive more without imperilling the results which it is the mission of the Anglo-Saxon race to accomplish? And in answering it we should take counsel exclusively neither of our over-confidence nor of our fears; neither of our humane desire to give a home to all the sons of men and our commercial zeal to develop rapidly our material resources on the one hand, nor of mere prejudice against foreign races on the other. Our destiny as a place of refuge and a home for mankind is indeed a noble one, and the right of asylum should never be denied to purely political refugees from other nations; but we can be such a home only so long and so far as we preserve intact and secure those distinctive features which first irresistibly drew and still draw towards our hospitable shores the wandering footsteps of all the races of mankind.

This question is peculiarly one to be considered and acted upon, so far as may be, in the clear, cold light of reason unclouded by either sentiment, fear, or prejudice ; and such check should be unflinchingly applied to immigration as shall keep us always well within the danger-line. At the present moment it would seem that we have decidedly less restraint than is desirable upon immigration from Europe, and that greater caution is needed. We have been too hospitable to the anarchist, the nihilist, the socialist, the dynamiter. We gamble with our birthright. We have probably erred in the opposite direction of too much restriction and exclusion with regard to the Chinese. But who shall say ? Is there not apparently a natural law in the movement of races almost as fixed and immutable as the law of the tides and the planets, which carries us westward and carries no Asiatic race eastward ? Can we help mingling a little Oriental fatalism with our reason, on this topic ? Is it not almost manifest destiny that the slumbering but volcanic millions of Asia shall not be allowed to move in our direction, but rather that our civilization, moving chiefly from our own shores, from Japan, from Australia, from India, shall in time pene-

trate the heart of Asia and transform even that
stronghold of human conservatism, the birthplace
and nursery of the races, into the form and
figure of our modern life ? Nay more ; shall
we not in our westward course take darkest
Russia in reverse, and cause the glad light of
freedom to penetrate the cruel fastnesses of Si-
beria, and the advancing banners of democracy
to enter even the gloomy fortress of Muscovite
despotism? Who shall say what even another
short century may bring forth, and can our
destiny have been fulfilled in merely reaching
the Pacific shores ?

Our patriotism is bathed in a warmer light,
our national pride is touched with a finer fire,
in this Columbian year than at other times.
The nations of the world are our guests ; their
stately navies and ours ride tranquilly at anchor
in our spacious harbors and salute each other
in harmony and good-will ; we feel as never
before the universal brotherhood of mankind.
The Anglo-Saxon has indeed displaced the
Spaniard in the leadership of that mighty westward movement of trade, conversion, and civilization, toward Asia which the great Genoese
navigator inaugurated and which has been for a
time interrupted by his discovery of our inter-

vening continent; but the Spaniard, the Italian,
the Frenchman, the German, all the races of
mankind, are sharers with us in it and con-
tributors to its completeness. Our present task
is the peopling and transformation of this continent; but our final calling is to press ever
onward and outward beyond the westward
horizon.

As we meet on this our natal day to take
note of our bearings, of the rocks and shoals
surrounding our course, the night of uncertainty
sometimes seems starless. But it is always
darkest just before the dawn; and if we were
asked to-day, with the difficulties before us
which we have been considering together, what
the special mission of our race, in the democ-
ratizing of the world was likely in the near
future to be, I think we might well say it was
the emancipation of foreign trade; the indefinite
expansion and improvement of free local self-
government, especially in large cities; the friendly
absorption and assimilation of other races into
our own law-abiding image, tempered always
by the stern censorship of common sense upon
the question of immigration, and by a dash of
superstition at the point where our youngest
civilization touches the oldest in the world.

With this noble mission and its responsibilities always in mind, with a national type ever slowly changing, developing, and improving, yet ever the same in the essential points of character and institutions, adopting and retaining such traits of other races as will enrich, vary, and enliven our own Anglo-Saxon heritage without imperiling it, and no others, we may feel on each annual recurrence of this day — forever the foremost one in our calendar — that there is no limit to the worlds yet remaining for us to conquer or to the latent genius of our people for peacefully conquering them.

A LIST

OF

BOSTON MUNICIPAL ORATORS.

By C. W. ERNST.

BOSTON ORATORS.

Appointed by the Municipal Authorities.

For the Anniversary of the Boston Massacre, March 5, 1770.

NOTE.—The Fifth-of-March orations were published in handsome quarto editions, now very scarce; also, collected in book form, in 1785, and again in 1807. The oration of 1776 was delivered in Watertown.

1771. — LOVELL, JAMES.

1772. — WARREN, JOSEPH.

1773. — CHURCH, BENJAMIN.

1774. — HANCOCK, JOHN.[a]

1775. — WARREN, JOSEPH.

1776. — THACHER, PETER.

1777. — HICHBORN, BENJAMIN.

1778. — AUSTIN, JONATHAN WILLIAMS.

1779. — TUDOR, WILLIAM.

1780. — MASON, JONATHAN, JUN.

1781. — DAWES, THOMAS, JUN.

1782. — MINOT, GEORGE RICHARDS.

1783. — WELSH, THOMAS.

For the Anniversary of National Independence, July 4, 1776.

NOTE.—A collected edition, or a full collection, of these orations has not been made. For the names of the orators, as officially printed on the title pages of the orations, see the Municipal Register of 1890.

1783. — WARREN, JOHN.[1]

1784. — HICHBORN, BENJAMIN.

---

[a] Reprinted in Newport, R.I., 1774, 8vo., 19 pp.

[1] Reprinted in Warren's Life. The orations of 1783 to 1786 were published in large quarto; the oration of 1787 appeared in octavo; the oration of 1788 was printed in small quarto; all succeeding orations appeared in octavo, with the exceptions stated under 1863 and 1876.

1785. — GARDINER, JOHN.

1786. — AUSTIN, JONATHAN LORING.

1787. — DAWES, THOMAS, JUN.

1788. — OTIS, HARRISON GRAY.

1789. — STILLMAN, SAMUEL.

1790. — GRAY, EDWARD.

1791. — CRAFTS, THOMAS, JUN.

1792. — BLAKE, JOSEPH, JUN.[1]

1793. — ADAMS, JOHN QUINCY.[2]

1794. — PHILLIPS, JOHN.

1795. — BLAKE, GEORGE.

1796. — LATHROP, JOHN, JUN.

1797. — CALLENDER, JOHN.

1798. — QUINCY, JOSIAH.[2,3]

1799. — LOWELL, JOHN, JUN.[2]

1800. — HALL, JOSEPH.

1801. — PAINE, CHARLES.

1802. — EMERSON, WILLIAM.

1803. — SULLIVAN, WILLIAM.

1804. — DANFORTH, THOMAS.[2]

1805. — DUTTON, WARREN.

1806. — CHANNING, FRANCIS DANA.[4]

1807. — THACHER, PETER.[2,5]

1808. — RITCHIE, ANDREW, JUN.[2]

1809. — TUDOR, WILLIAM, JUN.[2]

1810. — TOWNSEND, ALEXANDER.

1811. — SAVAGE, JAMES.[2]

---

[2] Passed to a second edition.

[3] Delivered another oration in 1826. Quincy's oration of 1798 was reprinted in Philadelphia.

[4] Not printed.

[5] On February 26, 1811, Peter Thacher's name was changed to Peter Oxenbridge Thacher. (List of Persons whose Names have been Changed in Massachusetts, 1780-1883, p. 23.)

1812, — POLLARD, BENJAMIN.[4]

1813. — LIVERMORE, EDWARD ST. LOE.

1814. — WHITWELL, BENJAMIN.

1815. — SHAW, LEMUEL.

1816. — SULLIVAN, GEORGE.[2]

1817. — CHANNING, EDWARD TYRREL.

1818. — GRAY, FRANCIS CALLEY.

1819. — DEXTER, FRANKLIN.

1820. — LYMAN, THEODORE, JUN.

1821. — LORING, CHARLES GREELY.[2]

1822. — GRAY, JOHN CHIPMAN.

1823. — CURTIS, CHARLES PELHAM.[2]

1824. — BASSETT, FRANCIS.

1825. — SPRAGUE, CHARLES.[6]

1826. — QUINCY, JOSIAH.[7]

1827. — MASON, WILLIAM POWELL.

1828. — SUMNER, BRADFORD.

1829. — AUSTIN, JAMES TRECOTHICK.

1830. — EVERETT, ALEXANDER HILL.

1831. — PALFREY, JOHN GORHAM.

1832. — QUINCY, JOSIAH, JUN.

1833. — PRESCOTT, EDWARD GOLDSBOROUGH.

1834. — FAY, RICHARD SULLIVAN.

1835. — HILLARD, GEORGE STILLMAN.

1836. — KINSMAN, HENRY WILLIS.

1837. — CHAPMAN, JONATHAN.

1838. — WINSLOW, HUBBARD. "The Means of the Perpetuity and Prosperity of our Republic."

1839. — AUSTIN, IVERS JAMES.

1840. — POWER, THOMAS.

---

[6] Six editions up to 1831. Reprinted also in his Life and Letters.
[7] Reprinted in his Municipal History of Boston. See 1798.

1841. — CURTIS, GEORGE TICKNOR. "The True Uses of American Revolutionary History." [8]

1842. — MANN, HORACE. [9]

1843. — ADAMS, CHARLES FRANCIS.

1844. — CHANDLER, PELEG WHITMAN. "The Morals of Freedom."

1845. — SUMNER, CHARLES. [10] "The True Grandeur of Nations."

1846. — WEBSTER, FLETCHER.

1847. — CARY, THOMAS GREAVES.

1848. — GILES, JOEL. "Practical Liberty."

1849. — GREENOUGH, WILLIAM WHITWELL. "The Conquering Republic."

1850. — WHIPPLE, EDWIN PERCY. [11] "Washington and the Principles of the Revolution."

1851. — RUSSELL, CHARLES THEODORE.

1852. — KING, THOMAS STARR. "The Organization of Liberty on the Western Continent." [12]

1853. — BIGELOW, TIMOTHY. [13]

1854. — STONE, ANDREW LEETE. [2]

1855. — MINER, ALONZO AMES.

1856. — PARKER, EDWARD GRIFFIN. "The Lesson of '76 to the Men of '56."

---

[8] Delivered another oration in 1862.

[9] There are five editions; only one by the City.

[10] Passed through three editions in Boston and one in London, and was answered in a pamphlet, Remarks upon an Oration delivered by Charles Sumner . . . , July 4th, 1845. By a Citizen of Boston. See Memoir and Letters of Charles Sumner, by Edward L. Pierce, vol. ii, 337–384.

[11] There is a second edition. (Boston: Ticknor, Reed, and Fields. 1850. 49 pp. 12⁰.)

[12] First published by the City in 1892.

[13] This and a number of the succeeding orations, up to 1861, contain the speeches, toasts, etc., of the City dinner usually given in Faneuil Hall on the Fourth of July.

1857. — ALGER, WILLIAM ROUNSEVILLE.[14] "The Genius and Posture of America."

1858. — HOLMES, JOHN SOMERS.[2]

1859. — SUMNER, GEORGE.[15]

1860. — EVERETT, EDWARD.

1861. — PARSONS, THEOPHILUS.

1862. — CURTIS, GEORGE TICKNOR.

1863. — HOLMES, OLIVER WENDELL.[16]

1864. — RUSSELL, THOMAS.

1865. — MANNING, JACOB MERRILL. "Peace under Liberty."

1866. — LOTHROP, SAMUEL KIRKLAND.

1867. — HEPWORTH, GEORGE HUGHES.

1868. — ELIOT, SAMUEL. "The Functions of a City."

1869. — MORTON, ELLIS WESLEY.

1870. — EVERETT, WILLIAM.

1871. — SARGENT, HORACE BINNEY.

1872. — ADAMS, CHARLES FRANCIS, JUN.

1873. — WARE, JOHN FOTHERGILL WATERHOUSE.

1874. — FROTHINGHAM, RICHARD.

1875. — CLARKE, JAMES FREEMAN.

[14] Probably four editions were printed in 1857. (Boston: Office Boston Daily Bee. 60 pp.) Not until November 22, 1864, was Mr. Alger asked by the City to furnish a copy for publication. He granted the request, and the first official edition (J. E. Farwell & Co., 1864. 53 pp.) was then issued. It lacks the interesting preface and appendix of the early editions.

[15] There is another edition. (Boston: Ticknor & Fields, 1859. 69 pp.) A third (Boston: Rockwell & Churchill, 1882. 46 pp.) omits the dinner at Faneuil Hall, the correspondence and events of the celebration.

[16] There is a preliminary edition of twelve copies. (J. E. Farwell & Co., 1863. (7), 71 pp.) It is "the first draft of the author's address, turned into larger, legible type, for the sole purpose of rendering easier its public delivery." It was done by "the liberality of the City Authorities," and is, typographically, the handsomest of these orations. This re sulted in the large-paper 75-page edition, printed from the same type as the 71-page edition, but modified by the author. It is printed "by order of the Common Council." The regular edition is in 60 pp., octavo size.

1876. — Winthrop, Robert Charles.[17]

1877. — Warren, William Wirt.

1878. — Healy, Joseph.

1879. — Lodge, Henry Cabot.

1880. — Smith, Robert Dickson.[18]

1881. — Warren, George Washington. " Our Republic — Liberty and Equality Founded on Law."

1882. — Long, John Davis.

1883. — Carpenter, Henry Bernard. "American Character and Influence."

1884. — Shepard, Harvey Newton.

1885. — Gargan, Thomas John.

1886. — Williams, George Frederick.

1887. — Fitzgerald, John Edward.

1888. — Dillaway, William Edward Lovell.

1889. — Swift, John Lindsay.[19] " The American Citizen."

1890. — Pillsbury, Albert Enoch. "" Public Spirit."

1891. — Quincy, Josiah.[20] " The Coming Peace."

1892. — Murphy, John Robert.

1893. — Putnam, Henry Ware. " The Mission of our People."

---

[17] There is a large-paper edition of fifty copies printed from this type, and also an edition from the press of John Wilson & Son, 1876. 55 pp. 8º.

[18] On Samuel Adams, a statue of whom, by Miss Anne Whitney, had just been completed for the City. A photograph of the statue is added.

[19] Contains a bibliography of Boston Fourth of July orations, from 1783 to 1889 inclusive, compiled by Lindsay Swift, of the Boston Public Library.

[20] Reprinted by the American Peace Society.

www.ingramcontent.com/pod-product-compliance
Lightning Source LLC
Chambersburg PA
CBHW031802090426
42739CB00008B/1121